Reliquary

Reliquary

Poetry of the First World War

Henry Smalley Sarson

Edited and with an introduction by
Alan Bishop

Rock's Mills Press
Oakville, Ontario
2019

Published by

Rock's Mills Press

www.rocksmillspress.com

From Field and Hospital first published 1916
A Reliquary of War first published 1937
Material new to this edition copyright © 2019 by Alan Bishop

Published by arrangement with the editor. This collected edition of the poems and prose of Henry Smalley Sarson, edited by Alan Bishop, was authorized by the author's son, Desmond Sarson.

For information, contact us at: customer.service@rocksmillspress.com

Contents

Editor's Introduction

Who has heard of Henry Smalley Sarson? His name does not appear in standard histories and critical assessments of Canadian poetry; and it is doubtful whether a single copy of *From Field and Hospital*, his slim volume of poetry published in December 1916, could be located anywhere in Canada.

Yet Sarson's war-poetry has been praised by the critic D.S.R. Welland in his study of Wilfred Owen, the great British poet of the First World War, for achieving "objective realism" in "The Village" and other poems. Indeed, the best of Sarson's war-poems are undoubtedly among the finest written by a Canadian, and should be widely known.

My curiosity about this little-known poet was not easily or quickly satisfied. With some difficulty, a copy of *From Field and Hospital* was located for me, nearly forty years ago – in an American library. I was sufficiently impressed by its contents to try to find out more about Sarson than the two facts revealed in that book: he had been a Private in the First Canadian Contingent, and had been injured while on active service.

A letter to the Canadian Forces Records Office in Ottawa brought me an outline of his military record. Born in London, England, on 16 August 1890, 33446 Private Henry Smalley Sarson had enlisted at Calgary in the No. 3 Field Ambulance, Canadian Military Corps, on 12 August 1914. After a training-period in England, he was sent to France on 1 July 1915. And from January 1916 until his discharge ten months later, as "no longer fit for war service", he had been a patient in several hospitals for wounded Canadian servicemen.

How to find out more? The Records Office could give me one important lead: his English address in 1921. With the help of a parish priest, and then of British Vinegars Limited, I was put in touch with the poet's son Desmond, of Wark, Northumberland; and at last could learn more about Henry Smalley Sarson.

He was a member of a prominent vinegar-making family. After studying at an agricultural college, he quarrelled with his father over the size of his allowance, and, a few years before War broke out, emigrated to Canada at the age of twenty-two. He spent some months in Ontario, working on a ranch and breaking-in horses for the RCMP, then moved on to the West, where he worked on the construction of a hotel at Lake Louise in the Rockies, and played piano-accompaniments for silent films in Calgary. When the War broke out in Europe, he volunteered for service immediately (12 August 1914). He embarked for Britain on 7 October 1914, and "proceeded to France" nine months later as a Private in the Canadian Expeditionary Force. In January 1916, he was "admitted (sick) to No. 7 General Hospital, St Omer, France" and, after being "Invalided to Britain March 5, 1916", was admitted to the "Duchess of Connaught Canadian Red Cross Hospital" and then "Granville Canadian Special Hospital, Ramsgate", and finally, "Being no longer physically fit for war service, he was discharged at Bath, England October 4, 1916". His Service Awards were the 1914–15 Star, British War Medal, and Victory Medal.

During his War service, Sarson had used his literary and musical talents to write skits, for performance by his Regiment's Minstrel Troupe, as well as poems, some published in military magazines. After he was gassed during the Battle of Ypres – so severely that he suffered from a damaged heart for the rest of his life – he continued to write poems. A selection of these, written behind the front line, as well as during his only leave and while in hospital, was published in London as *From Field and Hospital*, during 1916, in a series titled "The War in Poetry". They were praised as "powerful war poems" inspired by "the grim realities of war".

After the War, Sarson did not return to Canada. Now married, and settled into management of the family vinegar business, he wrote several plays, some of them successfully produced in provincial theatres (the outbreak of the Second World War prevented the production of one in London). But – although he lived into his seventies – he seems to have written no more poetry. The Preface he wrote for *A Reliquary of War* (reproduced below) suggests that poetic composition had become too closely associated with war memories that he, like so many of his fellow ex-combatants, found painful.

In 1937, however, Sarson had opened "an old trunk full of lumber", and found the poems he had written more than twenty years earlier – love-poems as well as war-poems. He decided to select the best of them for publication together with *From Field and Hospital*, primarily as a gift for his children. He called it *A Reliquary of War*.

The present extensive selection of Sarson's poetry is from that volume, with the addition of a few pieces that appeared in the wartime periodicals *Now and Then* and *Canada in Khaki* (the latter an annual anthology of writing by members of "the Overseas Military Forces of Canada").

These poems, many composed while Sarson was in hospital after being gassed, respond primarily to early years of the War (1915–16) on the Western Front. They are predominantly conventional in form and diction, but his later poems (notably "Anaesthetic") epitomise a modernist shift in Sarson's poetic writing, at least partly under the pressure of intense emotion. Also notable is his deep empathy for the suffering of civilians – especially Belgian refugees he had encountered. Forceful and direct in thought and diction, generally conventional in form and structure, Sarson's poems compose an impressive record of his experiences in the Great War.

In his Preface to *A Reliquary of War*, written not long before the outbreak of the Second World War, he wrote "I lost any idea I ever had about the glory of fighting … war is painful, degrading, and above all futile…."

Alan Bishop
1 January 2019

Author's Preface
'On Opening an Old Trunk'

Twenty years. Twenty years since these verses were written, years of varying fortune. Perhaps that's why I find them interesting. Relics of the past.

Scrawled on odd scraps of paper, backs of envelopes, and in cheap note-books, unearthing them from an old trunk full of lumber was rather an experience. The pleasure of the unexpected. What shall I find next?

Good heavens! Did I write that?

Twenty years is a long time. A business man gets a shock when he looks back at a pale slip of a boy who thought and felt like a poet and possibly was one. But it's a good shock, like a cold shower, painful but invigorating.

Obviously I was very much in love and love seems to have affected me with a sadness, a wistfulness that my success in the gentle art in no way warranted.

But perhaps that's why I was successful. And what a way for a soldier fighting for king and country to spend his time. Surely the worst place to write a love-lyric is an advance dressing-station or dugout? Or am I wrong? Maybe it's the best place. After all, Spenser wrote the *Faerie Queene* during an Irish campaign that must have been for him as bad as Flanders, so why should not a lesser one follow so rare an example?

I find the cynicism behind the war verses illuminating. I lost any idea I ever had about the glory of fighting very quickly. And marching side by side with this cynical outlook was a profound desire to forget all about it. To bury my soul in legend and romance. A pathological case, eh?

The songs and ballads for the Pilgrim Poet were done during the winter of '16 and '17 when Dodwell and I, both invalided from the army, were living on short commons and high ambitions writing a romantic novel about gipsies, highwaymen, and love's young dream. Alas! It was never finished. He, good soul that he was, scurried back to Canada when funds ran low, for we soon learnt that being literary gents and earning a living were two entirely different things. I wonder what's happened to him?

Some of them appeared in different papers at the time and a dozen or more made a timid bow as a 'Volume'. At the price of a shilling it wasn't worth it, though I have indisputable evidence that at least fifteen copies were sold. And once, more recently, I opened the pages of a swagger weekly, to find an illustration of the Cloth-hall at Ypres with a quotation from 'The Village' underneath. My heart swelled with pride till I noticed they had carefully avoided mentioning from where the quotation came! So much for fame!

And now I've dug them out. Perhaps some time in the future, when I am just dust and fading memory, you will read them and smile, and if when smiling you also realize, however dimly, that war is painful, degrading, and above all futile, they will not have been written in vain.

To Desmond, David, and Hilary
Christmas, 1937

Dedication

Do not forget as you forgot before,
Pray memory will live forever more
To honour those who passed the open door:
Do not forget the sons your Mother bore.

BEFORE

I heard a blackbird calling,
      And then the coo of a dove,
Soft, liquid notes were falling
      From a thrush's song of love,
Where daffodils were strewing
      Their golden poem to spring.
And I, who went a-wooing …
      Was hoarse and could not sing!

Perhaps some day the fragile ship I steer
      Upon a treacherous and sullen sea
Will drift into a fragrant harbour, clear
      Of all life's trouble, pain, and misery.

Perhaps a kindly spirit watching by,
      Seeing me striving, failing to attain
The end I seek, will lift my courage high,
      That falling yet I still may rise again.

Perhaps my lot is Joy and Power and Fame;
      Or yet my life may dwindle to its close
Unknown, unsung, unloved, even my name
      Lost in the dusts of failure: who knows?

WAR

The Armed Liner

The dull grey paint of war
Covering the shining brass and gleaming decks
That once re-echoed to the steps of youth -
That was before
The storms of destiny made ghastly wrecks
Of Peace, the Right and Truth.
Impromptu dances, coloured lights and laughter,
Lovers watching the phosphorescent waves;
Now gaping guns, a whistling shell; and after
So many wandering graves.

Twilight on a Transport

The ghostly mists creep inland:
From the sea as sundown fades away,
The purple cloak of soft approaching night
Hides the brilliant hues of brighter day.
The waves sing lullaby,
Murmuring love-songs to the swaying grass;
You catch the pathos of a plover's cry,
Night-haunting music; drifting sounds that pass
Into the mirage of Eternity.

St Nazaire.
February, 1915.

The Guns of La Bassée

The clouds ride up from the distant main,
      Hiding the moon's pale glow;
The wind, with the voice of a million slain,
      Howls a wild tale of woe:
While the guns are singing, 'Repay! Repay!'
On the road that leads to La Bassée.

The ruins of many a noble spire
      Re-echo the awful sound,
Where shadows, cast by the distant fire,
      Dance on the sodden ground
To the tune of the guns, 'Repay! Repay!'
On the road that leads to La Bassée.

A peasant, seeing the blinding flash,
      Mutters the Virgin's name;
He has felt the sting of the tyrant's lash,
      And knows of his daughter's shame,
So blesses the guns, 'Repay! Repay!'
On the road that leads to La Bassée.

For the guns are true, the guns are strong,
      And thunder-throated swell;
Singing their never-ending song,
      The chant of the flying shell,
'Repay, Repay, Repay, Repay!'
On the road that leads to La Bassée.

Estaires.
March, 1915.

The Refugee

The cobbled yard, with rustling poplars lined,
Stretches before me, reaches back behind
Where fields, dyke-bordered, lie dusty and bare,
Shimmering and dancing in the glare.
Breaking the silence of the noonday heat,
A piteous shuffling of weary feet,
An infant's cry, a child that's lost and calls,
A sob as some poor tired cripple falls;
I watch, the tide of sorrow onward runs
To the accompaniment of distant guns.

An old man white with age, a year-old bride,
Her younger sister trembling at her side;
A mother with her family of four
Staring dry-eyed, trudging on before
Her boy, who walks as going to the grave,
Pushing a cart with all that they could save,
Sticks and a chair, a jug, a crust of bread,
The only things they rescued from the dead;
Such are the sights that make my heart recoil,
Blocking the roads that lead from Belgian soil.

They never smile, these peasants passing by,
They do not laugh or chatter as they fly
And leave their homes in the invaders' hand,
Whilst they beg succour from an alien land.
Sometimes a wife, with red and swollen eyes,
Scarce noting her baby's piteous cries,
Will sob her tale of sorrow, but no smile
Will greet you as they flee mile after mile;
Forever with the hapless traveller runs
The distant muttering of giant guns.

A farmer's cart, its heavy swaying load
Threatening to fall upon the cobbled road,

Passes; the child perched high upon the top
Cries to the jaded steed if it should stop;
The farmer and his wife, a dog or so,
Follow; though they know not where they go.
And then a girl, alone, clutched to her breast
Her few possessions; onward she hurries lest
She, too, should perish; I try to calm her fears.
This is her tale of misery and tears:

In happiness they lived, life was a game,
Six months ago, and then the Germans came.
Her father and her brothers faced the foe,
She had not seen them since and did not know
If they were living or if they were dead;
Her mother and her three young sisters fled
To seek whatever comfort they could find,
Leaving all they loved and prized behind;
Yet one by one they died, and now bereft
Of all her family, she alone was left.

She told me of her home, the tiny farm
Nestling amongst the trees, rich with the charm
That only years of care and toil can bring;
How every morn the convent bells would ring
And wake them, to a day untinged with care:
Now, only blackened walls were standing there,
The crumbling bricks lay scattered all around,
A few charred rafters rotting on the ground,
A rusty plough, some broken garden tools,
Left by the lust of Kings, the greed of Fools.

She had a lover. Ah! her eyes grew dim,
Her lips, in anguish, showed her thoughts of him;
As children together often they would play,
Till growing passion chased their games away
And left them shy, scarce knowing what to do,
Longing yet finding not the way to woo.

Becoming bolder as the years passed,
She yielded her red lips to him at last
As his betrothed, his wife she would have been;
Then gruesome war thrust its sword between.

And so she goes – to join the crowd again,
The crowd of refugees that search in vain,
And I am left alone to ponder long
Upon their misery, upon their wrong.
I told her, 'God will set your country free.'
'God! There is no God,' she answered me.
And so the more I think, the more perplexed
My mind becomes, till lastly, sorely vexed,
I write the evidence for all to see:
The sorrows of a Belgian Refugee.

Vlamertinghe and Poveringhe.
April, 1915.

To a Young Belgian Girl

Child into a woman growing,
     Standing on the brink of life,
Is the stream so easy flowing
     That you take no heed of strife?

Dancing, joyous-eyed! Hard sorrow
     Cannot then, nor tyrant sway,
Crush your faith in the to-morrow,
     That you still can laugh and play.

Faith, unsoiled, that you will vanquish,
     Fortifies your breast to-night,
Though your brothers die in anguish
     In the thickest of the fight.

Laugh, then, though your heart is breaking,
     Though the tears fall thick and fast;
So 'twill be a pleasant waking
     When your faith's redeemed at last.

               Vlamertinghe.
               April, 1915.

(Written to a child of 11 whom we taught to sing 'Tipperary'. Three days later the village was shelled for the first time, and she was killed with all her family as they were packing up to evacuate their home.)

AT THE FRONT

The Shell

Shrieking its message, the flying death
   Cursed the resisting air,
Then buried its nose by a battered church,
   A skeleton gaunt and bare.

The brains of science, the money of fools,
   Had fashioned an iron slave
Destined to kill, yet the futile end
   Was a child's uprooted grave.

Elverdinghe.
April, 1915.

Laventie Church

Fragments left by a bursting shell
  Show where the altar stood;
A pile of bricks where the steeple fell;
  A Virgin carved in wood.
The crucifix, its burden gone,
  Stands awry in the nave,
The Christ lies under the scattered stone;
  Lost, like a felon's grave.

Unidentified

A wooden cross, guarding a patch of grass
And sodden leaves, seen vaguely as you pass;
Whilst wailing birds, wheeling the Heavens, cry
Their ever-rending requiem to the sky.

Mourned with the tears destiny decrees
The lot of broken hearts through centuries
Of dim uncertainty; unnamed, unknown
To us on earth, yet in God's records shown.

Fleurbaix.
1915.

Raindrops

Raindrops falling.
Falling on the reddened grass,
Where through the night battle held full sway,
Like Tears of God, that drop in pity, then pass
To wash our guilt away.

Harvest Song

'Tis harvest time, 'tis harvest time,
The corn lies stooked on the stubbled plain.
Scythe and sickle sing their song
In tune and time as they move along.
'Tis harvest time, 'tis harvest time.
We gather the golden grain.

'Tis harvest time, 'tis harvest time,
Red is the harvest we must reap.
To the whine of shrapnel overhead
The guns sing out to the live and dead.
'Tis harvest time, 'tis harvest time.
We gather that you may weep!

Laventie.
1915.

PARODIES

Rumour
(with apologies to Longfellow)

Should you ask me whence the legends,
Whence the stories and traditions,
And the wild and furious rumours,
That in never-ending numbers
Come and spoil our sweet existence;
Rumours of defeats and victories,
Rumours of impending troubles,
Rumours of forthcoming pleasures,
Growing like a mighty mushroom,
Travelling swifter than the swallow
Through the quiet of our billet,
I would answer – I would tell you.
Through the yard and past the cook-house,
Past the mess-tent and the washstand,
You will find a wall and doorway.
On the other side the land is,
Birthplace of all fearsome rumours,
Where they live and grow and flourish,
Coming thence in countless thousands,
To bestrew our lives with anguish.

To a Sodger's Louse
(with apologies to Rabbie Burns)

Wee scamperin' irritatin' scunner,
Hoo dour ye worry me, I wunner,
As if I hadna lots to dae,
Blockin' the road to auld Calais,

                    Without ye.

Ye'll hardly let me hae a doss
For you paradin' right across
Ma back, ma neck, and doun ma spine,
Thinkin' nae doot ye're dain' fine

                    Sookin' ma bluid.

When at ma Country's ca' I came,
To fecht for Beauty, King and Hame,
I read me yellow form twice,
But it said nought 'bout fechtin' lice,

                    Or I had gibbered.

When 'Little Willies' skiff ma heid,
Or me aboot to draw a bead,
I fain would stop to scart ma back,
To shift ye off the bitten track,

                    Afore I fire.

When through the shirt of Sister Sue,
I search maist carefully for you,
I smile to think the busy wench
Ne'er dreams her seams mak' sic a trench

                    to gie ye cover.

Whit Labyrinthine dug-out too,
Ye're makin' in our kilts the noo.
Ye're reinforcements tak' the bun,
Encouraged by the Flanders sun,

                    To keep us lively.

Gott Strafe ye, little kittlin' beast,
Ye maybe think ye'll mak a feast
O' me, but no, ye'll get a had
When next ye try to promenade

                    Across ma kist.

The mixture in the bottle here
Is bound to mak' ye disappear.
Nae mair I'll need to mak' ye click,
Ane dose they sae'll dae the trick

                    As sure as d'ath.

The Craven
(With apologies to Edgar Allan Poe)

Once upon a midnight dreary,
As I pondered, weak and weary,
Shiv'ring in my frowsy blankets,
Lying on a muddy floor,
Suddenly there came a tapping,
As of someone gently rapping -
Someone who was softly tapping,
Tapping at my dug-out door.

Oh! How well do I remember,
It was in the bleak December,
And no warm and glowing ember
Cast its shadows on the floor.
But the wind was wildly blowing,
Water through the trench was flowing -
So my grouch was quickly growing -
Wind and rain and mud galore.

Then the door was opened gently,
And I waited, watched intently;
To my boots my heart had fallen,
Someone groping, stumbled, swore.
In there came a mud-splashed figure,
Looking like an unwashed [digger];
With my finger on the trigger,
I was crouching on the floor.

'Twas the Sergeant with a jag on,
Reeling like a Belgian wagon;
Underneath his arm a flagon,
Which he pitched upon the floor.
'Sorry, chum, the rum's (hic) finished -
'Fraid your issue's gone - s'empty,'
Quoth the Sergeant, 'there's no more.'

The Sword

(A very dramatic sketch. It may be acted without fee or licence by anyone applying for a commission.)

TIME. - Three years, or the duration.

PLACE. - The ancestral home of a young subaltern, who, having been granted fourteen days' leave for the purposes of buying kit preparatory to leaving on draft, has just invested four pounds-odd in a sword.

SCENE ONE

– Curtain discovers LIEUT. X. standing in front of large mirror struggling with obstinate buckles. Sings:

A Captain Courageous of sixty-odd blades,
> All ready to fight
> By day or by night,
I leave every rival in love in the shades,
> To fret and to fume
> In perpetual gloom,
Whilst I steal the hearts of the prettiest maids.

CHORUS.

O, I am a soldier exalted and fierce,
I can parry in quatre, I can parry in tierce,
And leave every rival in love in the shades
As Captain Courageous of sixty-odd blades.

- Having extricated the weapon from between his legs, LIEUT. X. continues:

I can handle my man with the veriest ease,
> A lightning twist
> Of my elegant wrist -
So; I've skewered his heart and he drops to his knees;
> One moment to feel

The keen edge of my steel,
Then I sever him close to the waist, if you please.

Chorus again with vigour.

My noble Excalibur clasped in my hand,
    With *vivre* and *aplomb*,
    With gun and with bomb,
Then I'll marshal my men; at the word of command,
    We'll scatter poor Fritz
    To a million bits;
Or, point at his throat, on his carcass I'll stand.

Sings final chorus, making violent lunges at washstand.

O, I am a soldier exalted and fierce,
I can parry in quatre, I can parry in tierce;
Whether one against fifty or leading in raids,
I'll be Captain Courageous of sixty odd blades.

SCENE TWO

TIME. - Some two months later in trench 321 B.S.

LIEUT. X. *discovered groping at 3 a.m. in two feet of water.*

LIEUT. X.: Where the …. did I leave my stick? We're due to go over in seven minutes!

Slow curtain.

ON LEAVE

Love Song

Twilight, the shadows darken on the leas,
The noises of the day are hushed at rest;
Even the wind, soft rising in the west,
Falters and dies beneath the whispering trees.
No jarring human voices cry or speak;
       Twilight, ah, Sweetheart, may I kiss your cheek.

Night, a pale moon rises through the haze,
A nightingale trills in a thicket near
As suddenly night's voices sharp and clear
Echo and re-echo through the maze;
For twilight's hold of silence falters, slips;
       Night. Oh beloved Mine, give me your lips.

Bailleul.
August, 1915.

(Unfortunately nothing of the sort happened. But "twilight's hold of silence" slipped with a vengeance a few minutes later, when a Zeppelin, en route for Paris, passed over head. A nearby anti-aircraft battery cackled a perfect inferno, though nobody got within a mile of the silver sausage as far as I could see.)

The blackberries high on the downs
     Lie glistening in the dew,
Along the twisted rabbit-track
     Where I have walked with you,
And plucked them for your laughing mouth
     Until your lips were blue.

The blackberries high on the downs
     Were sweet a year ago,
When all my life seemed golden
     As the sunset afterglow.
To-day I could not gather them –
     Remembrance pricked me so....

After Leave

I held you suppliant in my arms
      And lost the world in love of you.
Of all your fancied fond alarms
      Were any true?

So soft and warm, upon your breast
      My pillowed head contented lay,
By your endearing arms caressed
      Till break of day.

We claimed love's heritage and so
      You soothed me as a tired child,
Told me your love, 'twas then I know
      The Heavens smiled.

Calais.
1915.

WOUNDED

To Sister E.W.

You gave me a white carnation:
      Was it in sympathy?
And did you know the flower meant
      Youth's glad world to me?

A simple white carnation,
      Yet you seemed to understand
What I craved was a woman's smile,
      The touch of a gentle hand.

So you gave me a white carnation -
      'Twas a foolish thing to do,
For whenever I see carnations now
      I shall always think of you.

St. Omer.
June, 1915.

Death's Chant

Are you afraid of me? Then see, I bring
Utter forgetfulness of everything;
Bury for ever in the age's dust
False friends, ambition, worldly greed and lust;
Until the generations yet to be
Can neither tell your fame or perfidy.

Life is so sweet? So you would crave to live
Receiving more than you can ever give,
Or do a woman's kisses taunt you still?
If so, then you have learnt your lesson ill.
The world will soon forget or never know;
Come! Kiss my lips, for I am Death: now Go!

Nieppe.
August, 1915.

Anaesthetic

'Breathe. Breathe deeply!'
My heaving lungs, scorched with the sickening fumes,
Mutiny, whilst the white-clad figures dwarf
To a dim perspective. Still a quiet voice
Reiterates, 'Breathe deeply, count with me
One, two, three, four, five.'
See! The room is dancing in madness; I fall,
Falling miles, miles, millions of miles!
God! What a crash when I strike the rocks!
Down! Down!

'One more kiss, Lass, come!
What a damned row those guns are making.
Get off my leg, will you, who's speaking?
What's all over? Oh! How sick I feel!
Who's that? Sister? Yes, I'll go to sleep;
I'm tired. I feel much better, thanks!'

In hospital.
1916.

I feel your arms around my neck once more,
         Gently your lips caress my own and yet
I know 'tis but a memory that fades;
         My eyes are wet.

I hear you softly murmuring my name
         Where daily a thousand voices pass me by,
A haunting melody of tenderness,
         A fleeting sigh.

Faintly I see you standing by my side,
         The ghostly phantom from a fading past,
You smile and ease my suffering, and so
         I sleep at last.

IN HOSPITAL

Firelight

Held by the magic dancing flame, I gazed
Into the living coal where changing forms
Cast phantom cities for my wonderment.
Chiselled of ruby stone in dwarfed prospect
Long avenues I saw, terraced with booths
Where merchants sold their many coloured wares
Gleaned from the East to eager, chattering crowds.
And distant hills, blue in the evening mist,
White marble villas on their verdured breasts,
With children playing, lovers sadly sweet,
Or grey-beards telling of their manly youth
To curious listeners.

      Poppies there I plucked,
The crimson border of a laughing stream,
Lazy, languid poppies; and I heard
Tinkling sheep-bells and the low of kine;
The scented air heavy of new-mown grass
Soothed my delight.
Then as a tiny spark fell in the grate
The scene changed; appalled, amazed, I watched
My fairy country vanish, the distant hills
Smoking with wanton ruin, and the towns
Razed to the ground, their marble red with blood;
The markets empty and the sultry streets
Slimed with corruption, rotted with disease.

      Then, slowly over all Time stretched a hand,
Till once again flowers grew in the courts
Where bees droned busily upon their way,

Merchants of an age-old heritage.
And lastly this, too, faded from my sight,
Only the glowing coals, my confidante,
Knew I had watched a nation rise to Fame,
Sink with Decay, and perish in Despair.

In hospital.
September 1916

Autumn Wind

Blow then, since you must!
Blow and chase the dust
That gathers: the last fading leaf
Twirl in a Death Dance, mad and brief.
Blow wind, sing the knell of Summer, chant my grief.
Sway the tapered branches of the elms with your might,
Blow, until the staunchest oaks groan in their fright;
Whistle round the eaves, haste your flying,
Someone sighs within for Beauty's dying.

In hospital.
St Omer.
1916.

Winter

The snow lies white in the field,
All barren and bare,
Whilst kites and ravens fly
In the winter air;
For Death, the drunken reaper, has passed by
And bloody is the toll that blood must yield.

The snow lies white on the ground,
Yet the soil is red
Under the falling shroud,
For Youth lies dead,
Whilst Honour chants a requiem aloud
And Pity shivers at the awful sound.

Bailleul.
1916.

The Fishing Fleet

The smacks lie in the harbour, clustered close
Like frightened mallards from the peregrine.
Green sea-grass clothes each keelson, barnacled,
Gently lifting to the eddying tide,
Fringing with sallower shade the festooned ropes
Mooring the captives.

      Folded and stored away
In gloom, dust-covered are the reddened sails,
A home for mice and cockroaches.

      To taste
The keen salt spray; then, bosoming to the wind,
Race to kiss the horizon, porpoises
Gambolling beside in glad companionship;
To ride again the heaving summer swell
Or drift becalmed in moonlight; feel the strain,
The fierce delight of heavy-laden nets;
The toiling, sweating fishers; naked feet
Threading the decks; an over-teeming hold
Full to the top, then home on sunrise breeze
To early market.

      Fading yesterday,
Lost in a vortex of world cataclysm!
Ideals of storm and shine, of wind and rain,
Mist in the morning, scorching sun at noon,
Beautified phantasies of green and blue;
Yet, now condemned in idleness to wait;
Dreaming by day, counting the stars by night.

In hospital.
1916

Murmuring at my feet the river flows;
Across the valley to the distant hill
The twilight mists are gathering; all is still
Save high in heaven where the sleepy crows
Cawing, return to roost.

      The meadowsweet
With heavy scent has laden all the air,
Mingling with the twining roses, where
Yellowhammers in the hedges meet
To chant the only little song they know
The whole day through, yet now they too must rest.
Thus you may feel the evening silence grow
And so are still yourself in wonder lest
You break the spell of twilight.

      Noisome day
Has flown and yet the night seems far away.

Cliveden.
1916.
In hospital.

ANGER AND SATIRE

Remembrance

Torture and tears to the fallen foe,
      Mockery, gibes and laughter,
These are some of the things I know,
      And I shall remember after.

A mother nursing her murdered children
      When madness had mellowed her sorrow,
But oh, the hate in her eyes was wild,
      And I shall remember tomorrow.

A boy with only one shattered hand,
      Wrists for your swords to sever,
'Twas long before I could understand,
      And I shall remember forever.

When power falls like a shooting star,
      Fades as a dying ember,
God! I wouldn't be what you are,
      For even the dead remember.

The German Spider and the Russian Fly

Oh, come into my parlour,
    Said the Spider to the Fly.
It's the finest little parlour
    That ever you did spy.

I will love you as a brother,
    In democracy we'll live;
And I'll promise all the pretty things
    I haven't got to give.

Oh, come into my parlour,
    I have vodka you can drink.
You'll have your votes and freedom,
    And you'll be allowed to think.

You shall have your representatives,
    And unions galore,
And other things you've never dared
    To clamour for before.

Oh, come into my parlour,
    Said the Kaiser to the Fly.
It's the finest little parlour –
    And he winked the other eye.

Two Fine Ladies

I saw two ladies in their car
  With seven Pekingese.

I know where your sisters sob
        The dragging hours away,
Where ever-toiling factories rob
        Children of their play.
Where squalid hovels, like a scar,
        Hide Christ's humanities.
Two fine ladies in their car
        With seven Pekingese.

I have heard a mother cry
        Her anguishing distress
That her first-born had to die
        To please the passionless;
And I have watched your children mar
        Their beauty by disease.
Two fine ladies in their car
        With seven Pekingese.

I know where your youth has died
        In suffering and pain,
That you might keep your honoured pride
        And glory in your gain;
And I have watched an evening star
        Weep for their agonies.
Two fine ladies in their car
        With seven Pekingese.

I have smiled to hear you talk
      Of statesmanship and art,
I've watched your self-important walk
      And analysed your heart;
I know you for the fools you are,
      Your puny vanities.
Two fine ladies in their car
      With seven Pekingese.

Hyde Park.
1916.

The Village

1914

Settling behind the haze, a molten sun
Clothes the distant spires in gossamer,
Touches the swinging windows of the street
With fire, splashes the trees in liquid gold
And, in lassitude of slow decline,
Heralds the twilight's ease.
      Weary Workers
Turned from the plough, home-trudging from the fields,
Smile at their thoughts of well-earned peace and rest:
For in the village bustling pots and pans,
Sweet pleasant smells of peasant cookery,
Spell preparation for the evening meal.
In doorways, taking vantage of the light,
Sit here and there a figure, busy still
With flying fingers, weaving spider thread
To fairy patterns of Valenciennes.
Children are laughing; by the tiny brook
They wander, playing, teasing, now and then
Tossing a pebble at a darting minnow,
Till women's voices, high-pitched to attract,
Cry 'Jacques', 'Noel' or 'Pierre', when quietude
Comes to the rippling stream, drifting sounds
Of laughter only echoing from the doors
Subdued in harmony.

Peace and goodwill are the master tones
Brooding on the happy evening scene;
The men, seated beneath the café windows
Talk, jest and laugh, with tinkling glass or mug,
And smoke their red clay pipes, sweet-smelling smoke
Of home-cured leaf, rising in pearly clouds;
Whilst women, some still toiling at their lace,
Gossip, the elder matrons of their homes;

Girlhood, as all girls will, so why say more?
For Madeleine, the minx, is missing. Where?
Henri, the cobbler's son, has vanished too!
Strong evidence enough for village life.

A pleasant word for all, a cheery smile,
And in return due reverence and faith:
Thus softly the twilight deepens into night,
Boy and girl have, whispering, passed their way
To the security of scented lanes
To dream – sweet fancies which the young enjoy,
The last thrush whistles in a distant copse,
As, only by the glowing of a pipe,
A smothered laugh, a restless infant's cry,
Is the blue silence of the Heavens broken,
To show the stars humanity still lives.

1915

The shrieking of a thousand maddened furies
Riding the air, a violent thunderclap,
Sharp, vivid stabs of flame; then falling bricks
And silence; deep, deep silence of the dead.
No other creature but a scurrying rat
Is seen, even the sparrows that last year
In cheeky self-assurance chirped about,
Have gone their way and left the desolate place.
In May the martins came again to build
Their tiny homes on last year's site, but found
The sheltering eaves where they had taken refuge
Strewn on the ground.
　　　　Those scarred and tumbling walls
Once were the church, yet might have been an inn
For all the signs of reverence they show
Save that in the encircling shady yard,
Heaped with scattered stone, the uprooted graves
And broken crosses speak of holier days;
The nave, choked with charred rafters from the roof,

Pleads untended to the wind and rain
Mutely; shelter even bats despise.

Standing stricken, the weary shrapnelled houses
Seem skeletons, grim and ghastly shapes
Beckoning with scraggy fingers to the sky
In silent plea for justice. A window gapes.
Laughing in mockery the frame still holds,
Grinning its execration.
      No solid roof
Stands to offer shelter to a dog,
Whilst in the rooms that once were clean and white,
Midst the accumulating broken tiles,
Grasses and weeds already have their hold,
Encroaching from the garden.

The road itself is seamed, pock-marked with holes,
Where you might hide ten men, nor see their heads,
Those near the tiny stream filled to the brim
With dank and turbid water; in greening slime
The bloated body of a puny kitten
Floats, decayed and foul.
      So everywhere
When yesteryear found peace and happiness,
Now death prowling lurks in gruesome power;
The thrushes sing no longer in the woods,
Whilst over all there meditates and broods
The sovereign cruelty of war.

Neuve Eglise, Belgium.
September, 1915.

SORROW AND HOPE

Cities of France

From blackened wall and rafter,
      From crumbling brick and dust,
From tears of joy and laughter,
      From burnished sword and rust,
From all that you endure
      From your agony and pain,
Your faith will shine more pure,
      And your cities rise again.

By crime on crime uncounted,
      By ravishment and lust,
By trial on trouble mounted,
      By murder of the just,
By servitude and sorrow,
      By the stricken and the slain,
Your day will come to-morrow
      And your cities rise again.

The triumph of your birthright,
      In honour of your past,
In joy to grant your earthright,
      In justice come at last,
In life made worth the living,
      In love reborn by pain,
In memory unforgiving
      Shall your cities rise again.

To G.

In the despondent fancies of my mind,
Bodily pain and anguish, mental stress,
Through all infirmities of feebleness
I pictured dismal fortune; I could find
In every little truant word unkind
In outward semblance, malice intent, till hope
Severed with doubt, parted, an outworn rope
And left me lacking faith, a cynic, blind,
Until you came, Light-Hearted Girl.
      Then cheer
Came with you hand in hand, you eased my pain,
And with your happy laughter cleansed my soul,
So day by day I watch, longing, and fear
You may pass on, though all my doubts are vain,
For I have tasted of Love's magic bowl.

In Hospital.
March, 1916.

Ambition

I seek no honours that the great bestow,
      No wreath of laurels for my brow, nor fame,
No blood-won glory from unfathomed woe
      For all posterity to curse my name,
 And generations yet unborn to know
      As tyrant – great, but only great in shame.

Rather, I'd live unsung by all mankind,
      A passing shadow on the path we tread;
Weary, a traveller at last to find
      A resting-place, unhaunted by the dead;
Where I could be to all things worldly, blind;
      And only follow where my Master led.

Bailleul.
1916

In Memoriam

Ten weary years have flown: I did not know
      Or realize the sympathy I lost.
Vain in my youth, I did not count the cost
      But silently watched you go.

Even at last you softly called my name,
      As though once more a baby at your breast;
Later, you sighed and passed, to claim your rest;
      Would I might do the same!

Ten years of memory, a little dust!
      It seems so much to separate our lives
When only my imperfect thought survives
      To guard the flame of trust.

> *In Hospital.*
> *1916.*

(On the anniversary of my mother's death.)

COMPASSION

Two Temples

In the temple of ambition
  At the altar of desire,
You will find the rulers waiting,
  Ever kindling the fire.
And the sacrifice they offer
  To the idols of their shame
Is the happiness of others
  Who know nothing of the game.

In the temple of contrition
  At the altar of despair,
You will find the mothers kneeling,
  Wan of face and white of hair.
There the girl-wife who has trembled
  At a legislator's nod
Is made holy by her tears
  In the presence of her God.

Bath.
1916

Bring roses for her pillow,
  With lilies couch her feet;
Bring cypress, yew and willow
  To weave her winding sheet.

We found her lying in a crystal pool
  Deep in the forest shade,
By branching oaks and lichened willows cool;
  There had she strayed
After the hyacinths we found
Torn and faded on the ground?

Deep in the pool she lay, the lovely dead,
  Her flowing golden hair
Turned to a rippling halo round her head,
  Whilst everywhere
The waving water grasses grew
As if to shield her from our view.

Caressingly they wrapt her tender form,
  Then gently touched her lips,
To place a kiss where kisses once lay warm.
  So passion trips
Sometimes, and cheating points a lie
Along the road where love and laughter die.

Bring roses for her pillow,
  With lilies couch her feet;
Bring cypress, yew and willow
  And weave her winding sheet.

(Suggested by a suicide. The poor child was pregnant, and her soldier sweetheart who had returned to the front was reported missing.)

R.B.M.W., Reported Missing at Passchendaele

My boy is dead: for how long have I toiled
Through dense, black night? You do not understand.
You take no heed! I saw, was it yesterday?
Girls laughing in the street; an organ played
Jingly, discordant sounds; and men cried out
In harsh, sharp monosyllables the news
And sold their papers.

      Someone spoke to me,
I felt – but then my boy is dead. Now all
The tiny pleasant memories of our lives
Come flooding back to me; how he would laugh
And cheer me; I remember, when he was four,
He fell and bruised his head against a chair,
Then cried until I kissed the tears away;
Now, he is dead.

      No! You will not sheathe
The sword until your honour is avenged;
People must trust the Government, believe
What we are told, but will that bring him back?
The day he got his Blue how proud I was;
He knew it too and teased me.

      Yes, of course,
You do not think it would benefit
The Allies' cause: I know, I read it all;
I must read something to benumb my soul,
For I am mourning, mourning for my boy;
My happy, fair-haired boy.

AFTER

Renunciation

If I were young as you are young,
       And all the world was gay,
Together we would love and laugh
       Through life's brief holiday,
Whilst Folly whistled in the wood
       A merry roundelay.

But I am old though you are young,
       And all the world is grey,
To laughing eyes and tempting lips
       I have to answer 'Nay!'
With only the memory of a kiss
       To drive my tears away.

Transformation

Turn your sword to a ploughshare,
      Make of your lance a hoe,
Scatter the grain on the shell-scarred plain,
      And banish your worries and woe.

Your tunic give to a scarecrow,
      Weld from your bayonet a scythe,
What matters a thought for those who fought
      If you can be merry and blithe?

Turn your gun on the wild duck,
      Cast your shot to the wind,
Dance you and sing, life's a good thing
      To all who are left behind.

Your haversack keep for your banknotes,
      Your helmet's plume for a pen,
Pay no care to the faint 'Beware'
      That drifts from the graves of men.

So in the distant midnight,
      With your sons stricken and slain,
To the victors' shout you will sob your doubt:
      'Our lesson was learnt in vain.'

Acknowledgements

I am very grateful to Henry Smalley Sarson's son Desmond Sarson, who in 1979 gave me permission, on behalf of the family, to edit and publish his father's writings of the First World War.

Unfortunately, at that time I found no interested publisher. Now, however, David Stover of Rock's Mills Press has kindly agreed to publish this edition.

I wish also to acknowledge the contribution of graduate students at McMaster University who drew my attention to pieces by Sarson that appeared in *Canada in Khaki: A Tribute to the Officers and Men now serving in the Canadian Expeditionary Force* ([1916], 1917, and 1919). "The Refugee" and "To a Young Belgian Girl" were first published there in 1916, and "The Sword" in 1917. "Rumour", "To a Sodger's Louse" and "The Craven" were first published in *Now and Then* (n.d.), an occasional news and literary journal, excerpts from which were given to me by the Sarson family.

In 1937, Smalley Sarson noted that many of his war-writings had not survived, especially those "scribbled in various hospitals during 1916, whilst the authorities slowly made up their minds I was useless as a soldier" (note to "Sisters"). One is grateful that some did survive, and can be appreciated a century after they were written.

Alan Bishop
1 January 2019

About the Editor

Alan Bishop taught English Literature at McMaster University for over 30 years, and edited several of Vera Brittain's writings, including her diary of the First World War, *Chronicle of Youth*.

Lightning Source UK Ltd.
Milton Keynes UK
UKHW010701301121
394854UK00002B/277